Leigh-on-Sea

Sailing Club

Boat Yard

Leigh Marsh

Hadleigh Ray

200 meters

DISCLAIMER
The content in this book is provided as a research tool and methodology
for engaging with the environment and provides no warranty of any kind.
The use of the recipes and its content is at your sole risk.

We do not recommend that:
  a) The inexperienced, untrained, unaccompanied or uncertified
     undertake mud walks in the Thames Estuary.
  b) The non-experienced conduct experiments with biological matter.
  c) Over-consume any found plant matter in large quantities
  d) Over-forage or regularly forage in the same areas.

Site locations of growing ingredients included in this book are for visibility
reference only. The majority of Southend's estuary is an SSSI (Site of Specific
Scientific Interest) a site of ecological conservation governed by Natural
England. It should be treated with respect and sensitivity. It is not illegal to
forage in the UK but it is illegal to sell foraged ingredients for profit.

Talking Dirty: Tongue First!

Recipes from the
Mouth of the Thames

**By Fran Gallardo
& Claudia Lastra**

**Talking Dirty events in
Leigh-on-Sea & Southend**

Mud Day and Leigh Heritage Day
18 July 2015

Fishermans Tasting of the Thames
25 July 2015

Open Jamming at Leigh-on-Sea
Maritime Festival.
2 August 2015

Fluids and Mud Science
(citizen science workshop 1)
15 August 2015

Tongue First Dining Experience
of the Thames
20 August 2015

Wildlife and Not So Wild Life
(citizen science workshop 2)
22 August 2015

A Public Tasting: An Evening
of Tongue Exploration
30 August 2015

Leigh Regatta: Chachacha with
Local Ingredients
20 September 2015

Events in London: Walking and
Sensing the City (a comparative
estuary/city citizen science
workshop)
27 February 2016

Talking Dirty Residency
14–20 March 2016

Invasive Ecology—a working group
17th March 2016

Explore the Thames Estuary
with your Tongue
19th March 2016

Foreword

Talking Dirty: Tongue First! Recipes from the Mouth of the Thames, is a commission by Arts Catalyst led by artist Fran Gallardo. *Talking Dirty: Tongue First!* was a series of public events involving local foods, their source, preparation and consumption. Following this the recipe book was produced in collaboration with the situated knowledge of South Essex people, scientific research and global socio-environmental 'trends'. This book contains instructions for cooking with estuary ingredients: Grey Mullet and Hair Soy sauce to inhaling Fogs and Airs of the Thames Estuary.

Through introducing local people to ingredients from the Thames in public cooking and tasting workshops in Leigh-on-Sea, they explored environmental and industrial changes including social impacts of these changes. Alongside these tastings, Andy Freeman led citizen science workshops which investigated the traces of waste disposal on the 'unnatural' nature reserve of Two Tree Island in Leigh-on-Sea with Dr Mark Scrimshaw, Reader in Environmental Chemistry at Brunel University.

Citizen science workshops involved the use of digital technologies to investigate the legacy of generations of industrial use and misuse in the estuary landscape to reflect on wildlife habitats, global effects of climate change, industrialisation, farming, risk and health.

Talking Dirty is part of *Wrecked on The Intertidal Zone*, an art and citizen science project to uncover and highlight local knowledge about the changing ecology, society and industry of the Thames Estuary. Lead by artists YoHa, Critical Art Ensemble, Andy Freeman and Fran Gallardo, and curated by Arts Catalyst.

Claudia Lastra, 2016
Programme Manager, Arts Catalyst

Contents

Introduction   05—09
Edge Cordial   10—12
Mud-Cola   14—16
The Invasive Flood   18—21
Slave Shrimp   22—24
Bivalve Broth   26—28
Vertical Commons Salad (including arsenic) 30—33
    with Blackberry Vinegar
Sea Coal with Bottom Feeders   34—36
Grey Mullet Sashimi with Hair Soy Sauce   38—43
Vape   44—45
Colophon   48—49
Index   50—51

4

Tongue First! the Tongue as the Site of Inquiry

The tongue and the estuary

How do we interact with and understand the Thames Estuary? This book seeks to discover and uncover the complex social and industrial nature of the Thames Estuary, through an investigation directed by our tongues. We invite you to use the tongue as a tool with which to question the complex human and natural resources present within the estuary ecosystem. Food, climate change, public health and the effects of pollutants, all are connected and can all be explored via the tongue. With the tongue and taste we can create interactions with history and the environment. The tongue allows us to gauge our molecular gastronomy and it can interpret the chemical world, for does arsenic taste like almonds? Does radiation poisoning cause a metallic taste in people's mouths? Not only is it a receptor organ for sensing but it also induces memories or a sense of place through neurochemical receptors.[1]

This book is and is not a recipe-book. As with any culinary protocol, it contains a list of ingredients and suggested instructions for the reader's own manipulation and use. Simultaneously it is a tool with which to investigate the scale, texture and experimental nature of the Thames Estuary. It is an estuary-essay, a seascape-criticism. This compilation of recipes emerged from a series of public tasting workshops and investigatory outlets developed throughout spring/summer 2015 that aimed to introduce and address the tongue as site of inquiry and exploration into the systems of biopower,[2] governability and everyday life which flow through the geographies of the Thames Estuary.

A history of feeding and the capital

The Thames Estuary is a heavily modified, semi-industrial natural environment that has maintained what could be considered a metabolic relationship with the capital: feeding it, giving it energy and dealing with its waste. It is both the plumbing and the larder of London. Before early road haulage systems, the east shores of Kent, Essex and Suffolk supplied much of London's greens, meat, herbs, fruits and dairy. From the 19th century to 20th century, barges commonly called 'Bovril Boats' [3] ferried waste from London to landfills and mucking flats: carrying with them the culture, dialect and politics of the metropolis. Today, five power stations flank both banks of the estuary, accompanied by expanding container ports, seaways and a lengthy string of historic landfills, many still processing London's waste. Beckton Sewage Treatment Works is the fourth largest in Europe and is the major tributary of the river Thames. The estuary still feeds the capital, now partly as a thoroughfare for fleets of ships transporting exotic goods, their emissions gradually polluting the surrounding landscape.

Vertical Commons Salad (including arsenic with blackberry vinegar, served at an Eco-Political Dinner at Metal, Southend, August 2015

Film still by Jim Smith, Zander Mavor & Alistair Oldham

Informed by a land centric bias, estuaries, wetlands and marshes were traditionally regarded as wastelands: uninhabitable areas that were a threat and obstacle to modernisation. Distant landowners such as The church and The crown reinforced this vision due to the impossibility of effective taxation and regulation of this highly productive and self-sufficient environment. Much effort was then directed into drainage and land reclamation in order to transform the spaces into sanitised and arable terrain. In stark ideological opposition to this, 'commoners' continued to make the most of the unique landscape, sourcing reeds for building, thatching and basket making; peat in bogs for pre-industrial energy and abundant fish and game for food.

The estuary remains one of the major wilderness zones surrounding London and has a vast capacity to support ecosystems and provide significant food stocks. The shallow waters, protected by intertidal muds, host cockles and oyster beds as well as providing grounds for juvenile species of bass, herring and sole. Despite this, anecdotal and local knowledge suggests that, for unknown reasons, these fish stocks are not maturing and have depleted in recent years.[4]

Two Tree Island, Leigh-on-Sea, as a landfill during the Winter of Discontent (1978–79).

Copyright Robert Hallmann

Two Tree Island and Essex

Two Tree Island in Leigh-on-Sea, the site of an ex-landfill now a nature reserve, was one of the main inspirations for this project. The island was used as landfill and sewage works from 1936 to 1974 and local people have long suspected the site of leaching PCBs (polychlorinated biphenyls), DDT (dichlorodiphenyltrichloroethane) and other contaminants into the salt marsh and North Sea. Little data has been released publically about what lurks beneath the uneven rubble but in 2004, the island percolated to the surface of the House of Commons following fears that pollution posed a risk to schoolchildren and had contaminated shellfish and other wild species.[5] Despite its neglected past, Essex Wildlife Trust and a host of local volunteers have done much in recent years to transform the island into a haven. Beautiful wild apples tempt you to eat them; blackberries flourish and cry out to be jam; fennel and sea aster spring from potentially contaminated soil. Should locals embrace the space? Eat from it, live off it? Or should they fear it? Scientific evidence indicates that environmental factors are important contributors to some chronic and common diseases, such as asthma, obesity, diabetes and cancer, all of which are prevalent in deprived areas of Essex such as

7

the estuary. The spread of contaminants from power stations, farms and landfill sites into the estuary habitats and then into human bodies, outlines the potential systemic ramifications of contaminant circulation in urban and ecological systems. The inviting wild foods sprouting from sites such as Two Tree Island become dangerous objects through decades of environmental neglect. They interrupt our wild excursions to challenge what is deemed edible and force us to acknowledge our more negative and damaging relationships with nature.

Food gentrification

Aside from possible toxicological dangers, the consumption of the estuary's natural produce and the question of who consumes it raises complex health and social issues. Estuarine foods such as samphire, sea aster, sea purslane and brown shrimps, which were once considered famine food, are examples of elevated cuisines, now found in high-end restaurants beyond the reach of many who live in the area. As accessibility depletes, so does local knowledge; as people lose their reliance on the estuary for food and work they lose their connections to the surrounding wild. Eating wild foods and foraging, spearheaded by celebrity chefs, is now seen as a pastime for those who can afford it. The tongue paves the way for gentrification, moulding urban areas into comfortable zones for middle class habitation.

With gentrification comes displaced and neglected communities, unable to access what was once their own. This extends to diet. Food gentrification has gained cultural and political attention recently; blogger Mikki Kendall remarked that "one of the perils of "elevating" foods away from their source cultures is that many things are not easily replaceable, or even accessible in all communities".[6] With communities priced out of shops and unable to sustain previously affordable diets, local produce is no longer an accessible resource. As gentrification seeps through the estuary landscape, deprived areas such as Basildon and Canvey begin to suffer from an over reliance on cheap and processed items that can lead to severe health issues such as obesity and heart failure. [7,8,9]

Disruptiveness and decisiveness

Climate change is altering the estuary: sea levels are rising, salt marshes are starting to erode and habitats are being destroyed. Higher sea levels bring us ever closer to these wetlands. The Environmental Agency,[10] in their 'TE2100 Plan', are attempting to remedy this rising tide-line by relocating or replacing 876 hectares of intertidal habitat over the course of the next four years. Although nature can be managed to an extent, it is difficult to predict the ecological effects of transporting new ecologies into new surroundings. Do we forget about

Two Tree Island once it has becomes submerged? Will it become unmanageable and begin to leach its toxins further into the estuary?

The estuary is a fragile interconnected ecosystem with historical, cultural and environmental complexity that resists attempts at reduction. Through remote governance, we understand and visualise the estuary using charts and data sets while local knowledge—held within species, landscape and people—remains largely ignored. The tongue, reclaimed as a disruptive technology, offers a seductive form of critique towards sensing and making sense of some of the anthropogenic changes happening in the Thames Estuary. Though we recognise our limited engagement with the area, we claim our tongues a valid form of enquiry.

Bon Appétit!

1. The insular cortex and the amygdala brain structures are important to memory function and taste, they give us the emotional flavour of life.
2. Biopower is a term coined by Michel Foucault, social theorist and historian, loosely the term reflects on the systematic control of individuals or populations by a nation state through an enforced political regime / technology.
3. *Bexely, Hounslow, Newham and Thames, were four motor boats, better known as 'Bovril boats' because of the colour and consistency of their cargo. Each vessel could carry 2300 tonnes of sewage sludge from East London's sewage works and out to the Thames Estuary to areas such as Barrow Deep. Dependant on the weather this would happen on a daily basis and continued from 1887 to 1998. The combined amount dumped by these vessels was 7.5 millions tonnes per year.*
Milne, R, (1987) 'Pollution and politics in the North Sea', New Scientist, 116(1587), pp.53-58
For further details: https://www.newscientist.com/article/mg12817453-700-technology-sludge-di...
http://www.shipspotting.com/gallery/photo.php?lid=146344

4. *Echo News:* "Sole searching for the truth behind estuary fish stocks", July 2014
5. http://www.publications.parliament.uk/ 12 May 2004:Column 343W—"Two Tree Island"
6. www.thegrio.com "#Breaking Black: 1 in 5 children face food insecurity", January 2014
7. *Independent:* "England's fattest areas revealed in shocking data that shows more than three-quarters of people in some areas are overweight or obese", April 2014
8. www.essexinsight.org.uk West Essex Children's Partnership. Needs Assessment, Children, Young People, Parents and Carers, April 2013
9. Food Poverty and Food Bank referrals. Research and survey results from the work of Manchester Citizens Advice Bureau Service, February 2013
10. www.gov.uk "Thames Estuary 2100, Managing flood risk through London and the Thames estuary: (TE2100 Plan, Environmental Agency pg 30, published: November 2012) "Sea level rise could cause the loss of up to 1200 ha of designated intertidal habitat in the Thames Estuary Plan area over the next century."

Edge Cordial

*What manages to live in
the ruins we have made?* [1]

Accidents afford a certain optimism. Britain's most valued wild resource grows as a shabby, short lived and opportunistic foul smelling weed. Its delicate flowers deliver a summer squash. Elder-trees thrive in derelict (private properties and old railways edges along the estuary) with parcels rich in human and animal detritus, where there are highly productive monocultures. Extinction is the business of the wild, it is the tragedy of wild commodities becoming a demand.

In the UK we rely on imports from Hungary, Austria, Denmark, the Netherlands. There are less elder fields remaining as orchards continue to disappear from Kent and Essex. While the price of 'wild foods' and herbal infused drinks skyrocket as we continue to rapidly service our wild palates.

1 Tsing, A. L. (2015).
*The Mushroom at the End of the
World: On the Possibility of Life
in Capitalist Ruins.*

Elderflower is a herb traditionally used as a detoxifier or for clearing the lymph nodes. It's also an effective and natural insect repellent and reportedly has a whole host of benefits, from helping with allergy relief to treating fungal infections, toothaches or urinary tract disorders.

Elder Flower

11

Edge Cordial Ingredients

30-35 full elderflower
   heads
16 lemons
10 oranges chopped
   and pared

5 kg brown sugar
8 ltr water
5-6 tbsp
   apple cider vinegar

Method

1. Fill a pan with 5 ltr of water and bring it to the boil. Then add the sugar, and stir until it dissolves into a thick milky mixture.
2. Pour the mixture into a large sterilised heat proof container. Then add the rest of the water.
3. Cut lemons and oranges into slices and place into the container along with the orange zest, vinegar and flower heads. Stir gently.
4. Cover and leave to slightly ferment in a cool, airy place for a day or two.
5. Strain the liquid through a muslin lined sieve into sterilised glass bottles.
6. Seal and leave the mixture in a fridge if it is to be consumed in the coming days, otherwise freeze until consumption.
7. The mixture will begin to ferment if you use non sterilised elderflower heads, giving it a fizzness, you may also use a small 1/2 tsp of yeast to activate this.

Recipe slightly modified from
the elderflower cordial from
The Women Institute (WI)

Collection points for elderflower,
Southend-on-Sea:

100g   51.536563, 0.633804
50g   51.536149, 0.633811
150g   51.537957, 0.633108
70g   51.537205, 0.634925
160g   51.536959, 0.639447
210g   51.536511, 0.639941
110g   51.535285, 0.635102
70g   51.545679, 0.655950
120g   51.540651, 0.653495
140g   51.541165, 0.644198

Mud Cola

From floating barges of urban refuse to mud-encrusted works of art. From the cryptic biodiversity of toxic landfills to the stucco facades lining the Shipwrights, in Benfleet, and other modernist buildings across the South-East. The marmite-like brown goo of the marshes is a constant presence and a point of volatile contingency in the estuary life.

Favoured by 17th century physicians, aqua omnium florum (all-flower water) was prescribed against ailments such as gout, rheumatism and tuberculosis, as well as for its mood-lifting effects. Its key ingredients were post-processed may-fresh marigolds, forget-me-not's, and other wild meadow flowers with which cows were fed. The source of all-flower water is belied by its less appetising name aqua stercoris vaccini stillatitia, or "distilled water of cow dung"[1]. The drink's uplifting effects can be attributed to the presence of the bacteria Mycobacterium vaccae in the raw material. M. Vaccae was first isolated from the excrement of an Austrian cow and is thought to induce neurogenesis: the generation of new neurons in the brain that produce mood enhancing serotonin and norepinephrine. As with other saprophytic organisms, Mycobacterium vaccae can also be found in the mud, dirt and soils of marshes and meadows. Our Mud Cola, like the original aqua omnium florum, uses M. Vaccae to boost the mood, improve cognitive skills and promote learning.

Mud is the new Prozac.

Mud Facts: mud is very calorific, approx 4 Mars bars worth (600c) of energy psq.

Sourcing ingredients:
Mycobacterium vaccae culture purchased from Public Health England:
www.phe-culturecollections.org.uk

Bacteria Collection:
Mycobacterium vaccae
NCTC Number: NCTC 10916
Current Name:
Mycobacterium vaccae
Original Strain Reference: SN 920
Other Collection No:
ATCC 15483; SN 920
Previous Catalogue Name:
Mycobacterium vaccae
Family: Mycobacteriaceae
Hazard Group (ACDP):2

Instructions for how to open an NCTC glass ampoule and reconstitute freeze-dried material.
www.phe-culturecollections.org.uk/technical/howtohandlebacteria.aspx

WARNING
Public Health England advises the following. All cultures supplied by NCTC, NCPF and NCPV must be regarded as potentially pathogenic, and be handled by, or under the supervision of, competent persons who have received training in microbiological techniques. In the UK this includes compliance, so far as it applies, with "Safe working and the prevention of infection in clinical laboratories and similar facilities".

1 Consequences of Sales Promotions on Sale of OTC—FMCG Products in Pharmaceutical Sectors Oct–2014 | Vol. 6 | Issue No.2 SECTORS Alexander CVJ Victoria* and Dr. M. Ganesan http://www.ijptonline.com

REPLACE CAP AFTER USE

BOC

TEAR OFF STRIP TO OPEN

15

Cube-Cola concentrate available from www.cube-cola.org, a project originating in 2003 aiming to produce autonomous cola from an open source recipe found on the web. Alternatively it can be made from scratch following the ingredients list below:

For 1 litre of Cube Cola concentrate:
.7g citric acid (C6H8O7)
.35ml phosphoric acid (H3PO4)
.05ml vodka
.05ml lemon oil
.05ml orange oil
.05ml grapefruit oil
.05ml lime oil
.01ml cinnamon oil
1/20tsp gum arabic
.3g sodium citrate (C6H5Na3O7)
.3g sodium benzoate (NaC₇H₅O₂)
.7g caffeine
.8tsp caramel colouring

Sugars: Isomalt has benefits, it causes less tooth decay than other sugars and has little effect on blood sugar levels hence why it is commonly used in sugar-free sweets. Its also used to make 'sugar' sculptures. Please note Isomalt should not be consumed in large quantities, it may cause flatulence or diarrhea (no more than 50g per day for adults and 25g for children).

Mud Cola Ingredients

10 ml of heat killed M. vaccae

3.5 ml Cube Cola Concentrate

150g Isomalt

150g isomalt

1.20 ltr still water

Or a soda syphon with Co2 catridges

Method (per ltr of cola)

1. To safely extract and use the M. Vaccae culture work with a professional laboratory.

2. Heat-kill M. Vaccae culture of 10ml in a Microwave for 15 mins at 150w to ensure safety of use of the product and no bacteria is spread.

3. Add 20ml of water to 150g of Isomalt sugar in a large jug or container. Heat in the microwave until completely melted.

4. Add the 3.5 ml of cola concentrate.

5. Carbonate the rest of 1 ltr of still water via portable carbonator such as a soda stream or syphon (often used to make cocktails and easily available online). Carbonation: approx 6.19g of CO caps per ltr at 20c using Co2 caps and a syphon, use. Recommended is this DIY method for carbonating water with: http://www.instructables.com/id/Home-made-Carbonated-Beverages/

6. Pour the sparkling water over the concentrated mixture. Not the other way around.

The colour of the Thames Estuary is mutable but on a field trip in late February Pantone 4485 gave a pretty accurate approximation. Pantone is a proprietary colour reference used in the printing industries, of the 1,114 spot colours available this colour was found by a marketing company to be the 'ugliest colour'. It was applied to standardised cigarette packages in Australia 2012. (*Is Pantone 448C the world's ugliest colour?* http://www.smh.com.au/national/does-this-colour-turn-you-off-20120816-24bf4.html)

The Invasive Flood (Semi-invasive Species Soup)

New food chains will replace the old.
Welcome to the post-native generation.

Smart phones, laptops, tea mugs and tampons all travel from the lowest-paid corners of the Earth where they are assembled and shipped to the de-industrialised world. The ships transporting them bring 'evil' interlopers who dare to spoil pristine pastoral landscapes after hitch-hiking in ballasts and water tanks, or attached in the hull of ships.
To keep up the continuous supply of your many screens and trinkets, shipping companies paint antibiotics onto their ships and so marine animals are flushed with disinfectants and antifouling compounds are applied to boats to deter them from interfering with profit (wakame, mitten crabs, mollusc's are among these cruisers).

Biocides now part of the aquatic environment are proven to form a toxic soup that is harmful on many scales. Commonly used are tributyltin (TBT), chlorothalonil, dichlofluanid, DCOIT (4,5-dichloro-2-n-octyl-4-isothiazolin-3-one, Sea-nine 211®), Diuron, Irgarol 1051, TCMS pyridine (2,3,3,6-tetra-chloro-4-methylsulfonyl pyridine), zinc pyrithione and Zineb.

In todays medical community antibacterial resistance is a prevalent issue. It has been discovered that these paints help bacteria form a stronger resistance to biocides.

Therefore, eating these shell fish and organisms, humans and predators may then ingest these toxic chemicals.

Finish your soup!

Ingredients (Serves 4)

30g butter

1 large onion, 1 leek, peeled and chopped

2 large potatoes — peeled & chopped (depending on how thick you like soup)

125g of each seaweed: wakame, gutweed and laver

100g hijiki

1ltr of vegetable stock

salt & pepper to taste

sesame seeds (optional)

Method

1. To prepare the seaweeds: wash all the seaweeds thoroughly several times, removing all sand and any lurking sea creatures and stones. You can soak the seaweed in water for several hours to remove some of the saltiness.

2. Because of its toughness the laver needs to be boiled for 8 to 10 hours so its fishy flavour is released.

3. After washing the gutweed requires to be squeezed dry in a tea towel. Separate and hang up the gutweed on a makeshift clothesline to dry it — this can be done overnight or left for a few hours in a warm dry place.

4. Blanch the wakame, hijiki and laver and leave to one side.

5. To prepare the soup base, melt the butter in a large pan, add the chopped onion and leek, cook until soft (approx 10 mins), add the chopped potato, then the stock and boil on a medium heat until the potato is cooked, around 15 mins.

6. While the soup base is boiling, prepare the fried gutweed: heat a deep fat fryer or pot of oil to 180°C, once at the right temperature add the dried gutweed. Please note the gutweed must be fully dry or water will react with the oil and splatter — causing serious danger.

7. Once sufficiently fried, remove safely with a utensil and to one side on a paper towel.

Sourcing Ingredients

When foraging for seaweeds it is important to keep in mind tidal-table. It is location sensitive and storms across the North Sea will impact the timings as well as the height of the tide. As a safety measure, one should consider returning to shore an hour and a half before high-tide, no later.

Invasive seaweed species

Hijiki (Sargassum fusiforme) Is a dark worm-looking seaweed often bought dry in Japanese supermarkets. The British Foods Standards Agency have not banned the food but issued warnings against its consumption, in its dry form it has high levels of inorganic arsenic which can greatly increase the risk of cancer. It is rich in fibre, calcium and magnesium. In traditional Japanese folklore it is said to give you luscious black hair.

Wakame: (Undaria pinnatifida) Wakame or Asian Kelp is a large brown seaweed invasive to the UK, it found its way from Brittany where it was deliberately introduced in the 1980's. It is highly tolerant and can thrive in an array of environments. It grows in abundance and forms underwater forests. It is the enemy of any mariner as it clings to ropes, boat hulls and can block water passages for drainage. It has been near impossible to eradicate however many are experimenting in the use of UV light technologies and heated water to kill its spores.

Locations undisclosed.

8. Back to the soup: Once the potato is cooked, add the wakame, laver and hijiki, cook for 5 minutes, take off the heat then blend until smooth, season to taste and distribute in bowls.

9. Season the laver to taste, with sea salt, pepper and sesame seeds (optional). Place on top of the soup.

Native seaweeds
Gutweed (Ulva intestinalis)
Also known as grass kelp it is a long bright green tubular alga which grows in rock pool and in estuaries. It also has bubbles in the strands giving it an intestine like appearance hence its name. It often grows where freshwater runs across shores and so is a good indication of healthy water. Kelp or types of kelp are rich in iodine and are known to aggravate thyroid problems and so should be eaten in moderation.

Laver (Porphyra umbilicalis)
On the Welsh coast it is traditionally used to make laver-bread (bara lawr), it has over 50 known minerals essential for our diets. It flourishes in nitrogen-rich water, as such it is found near sewage outlets. It contains sodium alginate which is used in mass food production as a stabiliser, it's even been known to form the pimento filling in olives.

Slave Shrimp

As in language, there is an inherent violence within food. This is the tongue's business.

Brown shrimp once would have filled the hold of many horsebacks and shrimpers along Hadleigh Ray but now their stocks dwindle. Populations have heavily depleted in the last five years and most shrimper boats are now up for sale. It's suspected that shrimp may have migrated to colder waters in the face of rising sea temperatures, nobody knows. When the shrimp were plentiful they were caught, cooked and sent to Morocco for minimum wage peeling before being flown back to northern Europe.

Shrimpers and peelers continue to be the disposable communities at either end of a miserable labour for the global demand for these tasty crustaceans. Now, Thailand is one of the world's biggest shrimp producers and can only keep up with demand by inflicting modern day slavery conditions on its 'staff' and tolerating human trafficking of workers. There also strange courting rituals imposed on the shrimp to reproduce in these factories. To stimulate mature ovaries and spawn in female shrimp, industrial farms practice eyestalk ablation. This entails gouging out one or both of the creatures eye stalks, the procedure leads to many negative effects including reduced lifespan of the female and eventual loss in egg quality.

Shrimp collection points

1. 51.525940, 0.64996
2. 51.526906, 0.661758
3. 51.527500, 0.672233
4. 51.529455, 0.665713

Fran Gallardo, using a traditional shrimping net made by Graham Harwood. August 2015

Shrimping Instructions by Fran Gallardo

Crangon crangon live in shallow water, is nocturnally active, while during the day, buries in the sand to escape predatory birds and fish. Fishing is predominantly done following the artisanal fashion, done on foot, in hip boots, with hand-held nets attached to a frame itself affixed to a handle. Push-netting is done over the sand in shallow water in spring, along low tidal area zones with minimal tidal force impact of off Hadleigh Ray. Individuals are carefully placed in a small pail.

The shrimp are gathered in baskets, the net is washed out and the frame is hooked on 'for' the trip back home. The catch is washed again, 'removing as much sand as possible,' before being thrown in the broiling brine. Once boiled the shrimps are no longer grey or brown, but red. The brine is poured off and the small 'shrimps/prawns' ready for the consumption. Shrimping is performed at low tide on a muddy beach with a push-net during summer or autumn months. The lower the tide, the better, with at least an hour either side of low-tide. Every two full moons spring low tides occur, which are the lowest low tide, and possibly the best shrimping time, location depending.The concept of the push-net is reverse to the beam trawler. While a fishing trawler drags a beam and a net, the shrimper pushes a beam or blade which is angled precisely to cut down into the sand or mud a couple of inches deep.

The pushing-net blade is ideally 2ft-3ft wide, acting similarly to a shallow plough or harrow.
The net needs to be pushed along, disturbing the beach bed under the cover of water, because at least 6in are needed for the shrimps to able to swim around, feed and burrow under the sand.

The shrimp detect the vibrations heading towards them and eject themselves from the sand becoming enveloped in the net behind the digging blade. This method works better if pushing against waves or current because water movement propels the shrimps into the net.

It is unlikely you will catch more than 30 shrimps in 4 hours in Southend waters.

Workers peeling frozen shrimp at the Dutch Klaas Puul shrimp factory in the duty-free Tangier Exportation Free Zone (TFZ). Klaas Puul have moved their peeling activities to Morocco in order to cut labour costs. Around 2,500 local workers peel, clean and pack the frozen Dutch shrimp and return it to Dutch headquarters without paying any tax. The average wage is approximately $200 per month. Juan Vrijdag / Panos Pictures/ Felix Features.

Method for peeling shrimp in a Moroccan factory:

Peel your own shrimps at the equivalent to the Moroccan rate per hour. MAD = Moroccan Dirham (Moroccan currency).

15 MAD = 1 kg of peeled shrimp (£0.987)
5 MAD = 1 hour (£0.329)

It takes aprox. 3 hours to peel one kilo of shrimps.
A working day last roughly 14 hours.
A minimum of 6 kg of shrimp per day.
Below that weight. NO PAY.

15,000 t (metric tonne) or shrimp still travel 3200 miles by truck to the Free Economic Areas of Tanger or Tétouan. Cargo is kept under benzoic acid and sorbic acid in climate-controlled conditions.

PEEL THAT.

Bivalve Broth

The UK's best tasting bivalves (cockles) are found in Leigh-on-Sea, they have been the staple livelihood for a few families for generations of Cocklers. Along the sea front in Leigh-on-Sea, there are rows of cockle sheds and fishmongers to choose from. Traditionally wooden rakes were used to gather cockles, however to meet demands and for more successful catching, modern day cocklers use dredging and water pressure to dislodge the cockles from the sand, taking mainly mature cockles.

Cockles and other molluscs have their own micro-production system of feeding. They are 'ecosystem engineers', as they filter sea water to feed from it (e.g. plankton). As a byproduct of this process they are excellent bioindicators for the monitoring of radioactive pollutants existing in the ocean. There have been many global scientific studies of the effects on communities and populations of eating radiated seafood (New Zealand, Malaysia, India, Slovenia and Wales to name a few). Polonium 210 (Po210), a natural radionuclide most commonly found in seafood and in heavy consumers of seafood.

According to the global data study by Lubna Alam and Che Abd Rahim Mohammed (2011), "the consumption of seafood can single-handedly contribute up to 10.38% of natural radioactivity to the public which is not a negligible amount." (1)

We should not stop eating seafood. Natural radioactivity or potentially non—natural radioactivity, can be found everywhere in consumer products and in nature. It is only harmful to health in particularly high doses and if consistently inhaled or consumed. Thankfully there have been no known reports of high radiation in the seafood in Leigh-on-Sea or Southend, so for now we may enjoy these delicious bivalves!

Images gifted by John Dickens (1989/90)
Above: John Dickens unloading cockles from a catch.
Below: Traditional yokes being used to carry cockles.

(1) Environ Health. 2011; 10: 43.
Published online 2011 May 20. doi: 10.1186/1476-069X-10-43

Ingredients (Serves 4)
1 ¼ kg cockles
50 g unsalted butter
2 glasses of elderflower
   wine
Pinch of sea salt or
   pepper to taste

Method
1. Always buy fresh live cockles unless they are
    pickled in vinegar.
2. To prepare, soak the cockles for several hours to
    remove sand and grit.
3. In a hot pan melt down butter, and add the
    cockles; followed by elderflower wine and sea
    salt to taste.
4. Cook on a high heat, toss gently to cover all the
    cockles in the liquor and until the cockle shells
    begin to open.
5. Spoon out into bowls and serve with
    steamed samphire.

Film still, James Ravinet

Vertical Commons Salad (Including arsenic) with Black-berry Vinegar

The Commons of Salad. Where there is mucking, there is grass! It will likely be a commons that seizes, eliminates or radically changes every bite of the acidic, crunchy, salty greens.

Wilderness has protruded from many wastelands areas, weeds will grow in concrete and some plant life can grow in heavily polluted terrains. Two Tree Island (once landfill, now a nature reserve) is a biodiversity haven. Samphire, sea-aster, sea purselane, fat hen and other delicacies spring from and perch on top of urban filth. They are the garnish of high-end restaurants in the city, where they are tasted with delight and command astronomical prices.

Largely, the Thames Estuary is an SSSI (Site of Specific Scientific Interest) and a conservation site. The mudflats are not populated or policed and they fall under what we consider to be the commons of the 21st century. Our shores no longer separate the land from the ocean. Rising sea levels, cyclic tides, geolocating satellites, atmospheric pressure and underwater building of offshore sites demonstrate that the shoreline is fundamentally vertical not horizontal. Sub-tidal marshes confine what lurks beneath the mud, but also protects the habitats and species from the foraging populace. Who wants to get stuck in two foot of mud when the tide is rising?

What has arisen from our 2015 summer of research, with local Essex folk, during our citizen science workshops, is that some of the salicornia also known as samphire (location: 51.53227115, 0.62600613) had elevated readings of arsenic from that of its neighbouring patches of plants.

The testing would need to be undertaken in laboratory to certify these results.

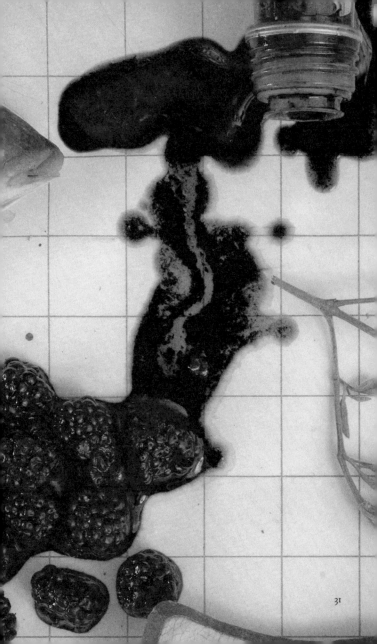

Arsenic is a metalloid; in large doses it can have devastating effects on human, animal and plant health, causing severe poisoning or death in some circumstances. It is naturally occurring in many minerals, in the 19th and 20th century it was used as a semi-antibiotic for diseases such as syphilis.

The main industrial use of arsenic is in car batteries and for strengthening alloys of copper and lead. These uses are perhaps why it has been found concentrated in areas of the estuary that are former landfill sites, however this is speculation until further scientific conclusions can be drawn. Samphire differs from sea purslane and sea aster — "salicornia plants can be a good source for the phytoremediation of heavy metal polluted saline coastal areas."(1)

Phytoremediation is the process of using plants to clean polluted ground, many plants such as sunflowers are capable of doing this. On the one hand, samphire is nutritionally good for us to eat being rich in vitamins and minerals, but on the other hand, environmental scientists relay to us, that they can also contain contaminants. The space between those two epistemes is yet again where the Thames Estuary can be situated, our mud falls between two worlds.

Samphire
1. 51.53227115, 0.62600613

Blackberries
Every year in mid August, after heavy rain and sun, blackberries appear alongside the railways of c2c. Train lines guarantee regular disturbed land for blackberry brambles to sprout and thrive. During the industrial revolution, jams were cooked using coal dropped from steam railways connecting London with Southend-on-Sea.

Berries were picked along C2C railways between the stations of Leigh-on-Sea and Chalkwell.

1. 51.541340, 0.643225
2. 51.536589, 0.635294

Marsh Samphire
It was used to make soap and glass in 14th century and was commonly called glasswort, sometimes called sea asparagus or sea pickle, it grows in clusters in rocky salt-sprayed regions along the sea coast and marsh areas. The best samphire grows out of mud that gets covered at high tide. Samphire is available all year round however foraging season is June to August, outside of this period the plant's stalks start growing thicker and harder and it is less pleasant to eat. Never uproot plants, it is recommended to cut the tips (4cms) as these are the most tender part of the plant and allows regrowth.

1. 51.537344, 0.645776
2. 51.537685, 0.643531
3. 51.537724, 0.646310
4. 51.537394, 0.640362

1. Anubha Sharmaa, Iti Gontiaa, Pradeep K. Agarwala & Bhavanath Jhaa. Accumulation of heavy metals and its biochemical responses in Salicornia brachiata, an extreme halophyte, Marine Biology Research, Volume 6, Issue 5, 2010.

Blackberry Vinegar Ingredients:

500 ml apple cider vinegar

450 g blackberries

Method

1. Place blackberries in a stainless steel or glass bowl and crush lightly with a potato masher...
2. Pour the vinegar into the bowl, stir, then cover and set aside for 5 days in a cool dark place.
3. Drain the fruit through muslin and leave the separated liquid covered for a night.
4. Pour the liquid into a stainless steel saucepan. Bring to the boil, lower the heat and simmer for about 10-15 minutes, scraping off any foam.
5. Leave to cool, pour into sterilised bottles and store in a cool dark place. It will last for a year.

Salad Ingredients

A scattering of
   samphire, sea aster
   and sea purslane

Method

1. To prepare the salad, pick the leaves from the plants or remove stalks, wash the Sea Purslane, Sea Aster and Samphire thoroughly until any trace of mud or salt water has been removed.
2. To remove the severe saltiness you can leave the leaves in a bowl of water overnight.
3. We recommend you slightly steam the leaves for 3 minutes to further remove any further pollutants.
4. Once ready and washed, scatter the leaves on a plate and drizzle with blackberry vinegar.
5. The leaves can accompany any sea food and also make a great starter.

Sea purslane
(Halimione portulacoides)
Its the carpet of the North East Eastern part of Two Tree Island and is a very hardy plant visible all year, it can be found in salt marshes which are usually flooded at high tide. However it is intolerant of waterlogged ground, therefore favours height drained areas. It is evergreen, and in the estuary it flowers from late July to early September. Leaves are eaten raw or cooked as potherb. They need careful washing when collected from the wild. It is recommended to collect max around 20-30% of the leafs on any stem. It has hairs to eliminate excess of salts stored in the leaves.

1.   51.537691, 0.644792
2.   51.538623, 0.644787

Sea Aster
(Tripolium pannonicum)
Confined to salt marshes, estuaries and occasionally to inland salt works. It has fleshy and succulent lanceolate leaves, with purple ray florets from July to September. It stays flowered until the autumn and is a great source of nectar for bees and butterflies. Younger leaves are preferred. Wash thoroughly.

1.   51.537344, 0.645776
2.   51.537685, 0.643531
3.   51.537724, 0.646310
4.   51.537394, 0.640362

Sea Coal
and
Bottom
Feeders

The Thames can be thought of as the larder of London. Before early road haulage the east shores of Kent, Essex and Suffolk supplied herbs, fruits, meat and dairy for much of London's markets. In addition to this a great volume of goods arrived by sea and river. Herring, mackerel, whiting and sprats travelled by sea from East Anglian coasts; butter and cheese from Suffolk; faggots and bavins from Greenwich. Sea and river were the main channels of supply; bypassing the congestion of London's internal traffic. The produce transported in the greatest quantities was perhaps coal, travelling on flat bottom vessels from Tyneside quays to the ports of Kent, Essex and London.

Many barges sunk in stormy weather and dumped their cargo on the Thames Estuary floors. While barges were worth £120 at the time, the coal cargo worth a mere £6, the cargo remained where it was, not worth a salvage mission to rescue it. Today commercial fisheries trawling for skates, rays and other bottom-feeders often haul up big lumps of seacoal (sometimes 20kg) trapped in the net. Cooking with coal is unfortunately common in the developing world, it is a highly polluting method that when used indoors over several years causes respiratory illnesses. Around one million coal-cookers are sold monthly in China alone which, along with India, remains one of the few places in the world where coal is the primary fuel for cooking.

Skates are similar to sting rays, are some of the oldest, jawed vertebrates in the world, dating back to the Lower Jurassic era (150,000 million years ago) they are flat, diamond shaped and cartilaginous. It's famous for its ammonia like smell, in Korea, this is utilised for culinary purposes, where they let the skate ferment in its urea, a delicacy called Hongeohoe which is feared for its unique flavour.

Fishing for coal and skate:
Coal and Skate Location:
51.499644, 0.959094 or 51°
29' 58".72 N 0°57' 32". 74 E.

Ask a local fisherman for skate
sourced from the coal barges.

To remedy this, it's best to soak the fish in water with lemon. To give reference to the importance of coal in the UK's past and to think about its ongoing dependence in the world, for this recipe we steam the skate using the coal that was caught with it, purchasing a Chinese standard coal-burner to cook it.

Image: by Jim Smith, Zander Mavor and Alistair Oldham, 2015 Film still, during *A Fishermen's Tasting of the Thames* event, cooking skate on a coal fired cooker.

Ingredients (Serves 2)

1 skate fish to share (225g per person)

water for steaming (dependent on pan size)

2 tsp alexanders seeds (optional)

40 g sea aster

sea salt & lemon to taste

Method

1. Quickly wash the skate to remove its natural slime. Be careful not to injure yourself on the spines that run from nose to tail and that fan out from the wings.
2. Find the connecting joint between the wing and the body and cut along it to remove the wing. Do this for both wings.
3. Skate must be skinned on both the upper and lower side of the wing. The upper side has a darker rougher skin and the lower has a lighter smoother skin.
4. Starting with the upper side, lay your wing flat on a cutting board and use a sharp knife to pry up the skin at the corner joint, making sure not to cut into the flesh.
5. Using a pair of pliers, grasp the loose corner of skin and slowly peel back diagonally off the wing. It should come off in a continuous piece but is slippery and often firmly attached so have patience. Turn over and repeat with the underside.
6. Cut along the outside edge of the wing to remove any spines.
7. There will be a layer of cartilage running between the upper and lower wing fillets, cook 'on the bone'.
8. To cook the skate with the sea coal you will require a coal cooker, commonly used in Chinese cooking. Season the fish with salt and alexanders, place in a large pan for steaming with sea aster for 15 minutes.
9. To serve, place on one large plate to share and scatter the sea vegetables on top, use a good squeeze of lemon.

Alexanders seeds.

Grey Mullet Sashimi with Hair Soy Sauce

History and stories of race, science, industry, and medicine lurk amongst hair's unsightly unatural, excessive or kinky relationships with the English-South. Salons proliferate as Leigh-on-Sea receives more wealthy commuters flocking everyday from London's financial districts. Who does not prefer estuarine views? Once a small fishing town sitting at the north bank of the estuary, locals now joke that Leigh-on-Sea must have the highest density of salons in the UK and have dubbed newcomers 'hairdressers'.

In 2005, a small-scale Chinese operation was caught using human hair instead of soya to make low-cost soy sauce. Until an EU ban in 2012, human hair was preferred over feather or sheep wool to source amino acids, simple organic compounds that form proteins. The sought after amino was L-cysteine (L-cys), used as a food additive or dietary supplement and in cheap ersatz dark sauces, where it adds a characteristic umami flavour. Nowadays, rather than hair, all L-cys is metabolised by genetically modified microorganisms.

During the summer of 2015 we prepared sashimi from grey mullet, caught in the Old Leigh using nets borrowed from town fisherman. This dish aims to question the deep and painful transformations many fishing towns have undergone during the last 10 years, from hubs of labour to gentrified salon destinations, and to learn the many stories that L-cysteine still can unfold.

Michael Meddle, a local fisherman instructing Fran Gallardo on how to fish for grey mullet.

M: *Mullets' still about? I haven't seen any ... but I have'nt been looking.*

F: *Graham said he saw some in the creek where the Souvenir was.*

M: *When was that?*

F: *A few days ago.*

M: *So we may still be lucky. Put one anchor here then I'll take one anchor the tide comes in this way. So this is the heavy end, if you*

put this over here—put that end down — like that, as the tide comes in this way, it's better it will just lift. If that's that way it will just drag, sometimes it gets caught. The tide comes in, obviously across the top. That's it, alright it's all gone out the bin. All I do with that is, erm, well the anchor's too big for this anyway so... anyway just stick it through there. When you're in a dinghgy you can just pull on this and it will pull [the anchor] out obviously you put the anchor on the heavy end. Just pull it out so it doesn't get caught, you can see it gets narrow there. The heavy end always goes first. I've never done it in the dark.

F: That would be fun.

Ingredients Hair Soy Sauce

(Serves 3 US cup or 0.709765 litres)

12 tsp balsamic vinegar	To ensure high
6 tsp unsulphured molasses	probability of human source for L-cysteine,
3/4 tsp ground ginger	please purchase product
3 pinch white pepper	with fabrication date
3 pinch garlic powder	before 2011.
3 tsp of L-cysteine.	salt, to taste (optional)

Method

1. In a saucepan, over medium heat, stir together all of the ingredients, except salt. Bring to a boil.

2. Continue to boil gently until liquid is reduced to about one cup, for about 15 minutes.
   Taste sauceand season as needed with sea salt, until desired saltiness is reached.

3. Store the sauce tightly covered in a soy sauce bottle, in the refrigerator for up to one week.

4. Shake before using.

Film still by Jim Smith, Zander Mavor and Alistair Oldham: Chef Jo Ryan preparing Grey Mullet for an Eco-Political Dinner for guests at Metal, Southend:

... Okay this is for, let me see, I think this is the penultimate course, this is a grey mullet sashimi, a fish native to the Thames Estuary, we'll be serving it raw, sliced thin, with a type of I guess, soy sauce effectively that Fran has made using human hair (proteins) and a sort of english wasabi which is made from some mustard horseradish and sea asparagus which a local collected herb, from Two Tree Island, which is just over there, somewhere. ...

About grey mullet
Mullet are thick-lipped grey mullet
have broad heads, metallic blue backs
and silvery sides with longitudinal
grey stripes. Their meat tastes
earthy. They feed on soft vegetable
matter and small aquatic creatures
growing in the mucking flats or on
yacht's hulls. They are slow growing
and smart, making them difficult to
catch by angling.

How to fish
The best technique to catch
grey-mullet has not changed
in centuries: a 50 yard gill net with
a floating upper line (headrope) and
a sinking lower line (footrope). It
ensnares grey mullet as they swim,
and ca be caught in the first and last
20 minutes of high and low tide.
Use a small dingy to load the
catch, collect the net and to go back
to the shore. Waders are used to
mudwalk along the net. It is
important to highlight that under
UK regulations only non-motorised
fishing vessels (regardless of the
size) are allowed to fish for
self-consumption.

Ingredients (Serves 8)
0,5 kg of grey mullet

Fish preparation

Filleting

1. Remove the scales with a descaler, running it
   from the tail towards the head. Do this for
   both sides.
2. Make an incision under the chin of the fish and
   from here, run the knife down the belly of the
   fish until you reach the tail.
3. Use the knife to scrape the guts out.
4. Cut around the fish's head and remove along
   with the gills.
5. Lay the fish flat on one side and cut along one
   side of the backbone from head to tail.
6. Once you reach the tail, turn the knife and
   run back up towards the head, running
   along the ribcage.
7. Once you reach the head, turn the knife once
   again and run back towards the tail cutting
   through the remaining flesh and the pin bones
   to remove the fillet from the body.
8. Turn the fish over onto its other side and repeat.

Location 51.540442, 0.647058

Skinning

1. Place the fillet skin side down and make a small incision at the tail end, making sure not to cut into the flesh.
2. Grip the loose skin firmly with your free hand and run the knife up towards the head in one slow smooth movement, making sure to keep the knife flat and level whilst making small saw like movements as you progress.
3. Do this for both fillets.

Sashimi cutting

1. Quickly rinse your skinned fillet under running water and place flat on a cutting board.
2. Hold the fillet firmly in one hand and using the sharpest knife you have, cut straight down into quarter inch slices.
3. A tip is to hold the fish right at the edge of where you are about to cut so that your finger tips are resting on the flat of the blade. This will allow for the cleanest cut possible.

To serve place on an oblong serving plate to share, drizzle on soy sauce to taste.

Vape

On airs (and smogs) of fruits and flowers of the Thames.

Canvey Wick is the site of a former oil refinery which was closed and partially dismantled after local protests and pressures. Small campfires and motorcycle races prevented large trees from taking over and the abandoned space quickly became a sanctuary for rare bugs, bees and an array of plant life. The Wick now has the highest biodiversity ratio in the UK, its greenery clouding a history of smogs and fumes. Elsewhere along the Thames Estuary one will find empty plots of land, the byproduct of un-affordable housing projects and the slow colonising creep of gentrification. These patches of disturbed land are havens for weeds and wild quick growing plants.

You are invited to taste and smell the fruits and flowers of the Thames Estuary that occupy these areas of environmentally embedded violence and dispossession. This is an inhalable history of air pollutants, abandoned space and opportunistic plants species that fill the void.

Puff it in.

Foraging

Our selection of plants take us around the estuary landscape. From roadsides, disturbed lands and former landfills, to the highest income neighbourhoods in the region and to the local courthouses that act as a battleground for so much of this changing landscape. Also included is the dreaded Japanese knotweed, enemy number one for urban developers costing £100 per square metre for it to be eradicated and is often injected with chemicals which if eaten is lethal to human health. Its location remains undisclosed.

wild rose 51.539131, 0.658161
use flowers mostly
sea aster 51.537537, 0.644308
ramsons 51.535035, 0.586911
common poppy 51.543601, 0.611946
pignut 51.542531, 0.638864
marjoram: 51.542464, 0.641976
common mallow:
51.539679, 0.654042
juniper: 51.540695, 0.653539
fennel: 51.537149, 0.629527
elderflower: see edge Cordial
recipe for coordinates
alexanders: 51.542006, 0.643210
mugwort: 51.536217, 0.632614
Japanese knotweed (classified)

Film still from film by *Jim Smith, Zander Mavor and Alistair Oldham*

Local artist and researcher Stuart Bowditch met Fran Gallardo to investigate the Estuary for edible plants in July 2015:

I met Fran at about 7am and we set out to collect a lot of locally grown plants for use in the meal that we were having later on the boat. We travelled out across the mud in our wellies all the way to two tree island & Fran's very knowledgeable about all the plants there so I learned a lot from him. We also found a lot of Sea including Sea Aster, Sea Purslane, and some Samphire, he was able to collect a lot of that, we also found a lot of other things—apples, horse radish and some berries which he couldn't really use in the meal later in the day but it was still interesting to see that they were growing there. Two Tree Island today is a nature reserve and a Site of Specific Scientific Interest (SSSI) on it's eastern end. But in the past it's been a tip and a rubbish dump, so there's all kinds of layers to its history there. Because it was a municipal tip for quite some time there is a possibility that the food can be contaminated with all kinds of different things such as arsenic and elements in the environment that could be dangerous to us and in the plants themselves so we will be doing some citizen science workshops and some tests on the plants to determine how much of these elements is present in them.

Interview originally filmed by Jim Smith, Zander Mavor and Alistair Oldham.

Ingredients (per plant)

1 tsp of plant matter to 150 ml vegetable glycerin

21 ml of purified water

Method

1. Mix kosher grade vegetable oil and purified water in a ratio of 7 parts oil, 1 part water.
2. Immerse the plant matter in the liquid and heat in a slow cooker overnight on the lowest heat setting.
3. Strain the liquid through a sieve before pouring into the vaping device liquid chamber. Vapes or e-cigarettes are unscrewed and liquid is poured into a chamber, make sure the wick inside is the chamber is moistened by the liquid before you try to vape.

46

Texts and research Fran Gallardo,
    Claudia Lastra & Eliot Haworth
Editing Claudia Lastra &
    Eliot Haworth
Copyediting Patricia Hallam,
    Finola Simpson & Diane Edwards
Recipe advice from Joseph Ryan, Chef
Advice and background knowledge
    Andy Freeman & Stuart Bowditch
Design Åbäke with Sandra Junker
Recipe book photography
    Sandra Junker
First person perspective photos
    Fran Gallardo using Go-pro
Typefaces Doves Type ℂ by
    Robert Green. Rail Alphabet by
    Jock Kinneir and Margaret Calvert
    for British Railways & Bruce

ARTS CATALYST

Published by Arts Catalyst
Centre for Art Science & Technology
74–76 Cromer Street
London, WC1H 8DR

Supported by
wellcometrust

The publisher has made every effort
to contact all copyright holders. If
proper acknowledgment has not been
made, we ask copyright holders to
contact the publisher.

www.artscatalyst.org
www.wrecked.artscatalyst.org

#tonguefirstinthethames

With many thanks to YoHa
(Graham Harwood and Matsuko
Yokokoji), Andy Freeman, Michaela
Freeman, Patrick Lacey (Åbäke),
Sandra Junker, Nicola Triscott,
Jessica Wallis, Alec Steadman,
Gary Sangster, Dr Mark Scrimshaw
(Reader in Environmental Chemistry,
Brunel University), Julie Peek,
Jo Ryan, Nastassja Simensky,
Irati Arrieta Vega, James Ravinet,
Warren Harper, Stuart Bowditch,
Oliver Spall, Leigh Town Council,
Leigh Heritage Centre, Joe Hill (Focal
Point Gallery), Metal Culture
(Southend), Belton Way Small Craft
Club, Leigh Heritage Centre,
Southend Borough Council,
Marc Outen (Essex Wildlife Trust),
Erika Wall, Fishermen's Chapel,
Paul Huxler, Norman Days, Shirley,
Michael Meddle, Steve Meddele,
Brum, The Fun Mud Day Volunteers
& John Dickens (a friend, lovely
smuggler, queer sailor and activist)

Supported using public funding by
**ARTS COUNCIL
ENGLAND**

Fran Gallardo's background is in systems engineering. He is a member of the Environmental Art Activism movement. Fran's work explores interfaces for culture in technology and ecology. In 2015, he led the Arts Catalyst project *Talking Dirty! Tongue First: Experiments at the Mouth of the Thames*. This was a series of public events including workshops, public tastings and dinners investigating the eco-political, historical, industrial and molecular networks of the Thames Estuary through the tongue and taste.

Andy Freeman is an artist, educator, technologist and former oyster farmer. Andy has worked with software and community arts projects and was founder member of the Australian Network for Arts and Technology. Based on his arts practice and his teaching at Goldsmiths College, University of London, Andy has developed a practice that involves the combination of open data tactics and community engagement.

Claudia Lastra is Programme Manager at Arts Catalyst and the curator of *Talking Dirty: Tongue First! Experiments at the Mouth of the Thames*. Since 2013 she has been working in Leigh-on-Sea & Southend, producing the project *Wrecked on the Intertidal Zone*, with artists Fran Gallardo, Andy Freeman, YoHa and Critical Art Ensemble to deliver a series of ambitious projects relating to the environment, industry and cultural changes of the Thames Estuary. Claudia joined Arts Catalyst in 2011.

Arts Catalyst commissions art that experimentally and critically engages with science. The organisation produces produce provocative, powerful, risk-taking projects to spark dynamic conversations about our changing world. Arts Catalyst plays a leading role in the development of artists' engagement with science, and critical discourse around this field. Through our commissions, exhibitions and events, we enable people to have distinctive, thought-provoking experiences that transcend traditional boundaries of art and science.

❡ THE DOVES PRESS WAS FOUNDED IN 1900 by T. J. Cobden-Sanderson, in partnership with process printer, engraver & photographer Emery Walker, in Hammersmith, London. During its seventeen years of operation, the Doves Press produced some of the finest & most notable examples of twentieth century typography. The distinguishing & most celebrated feature of its books was a specially devised fount of type. When the partnership was formally dissolved in 1909, a settlement was proposed whereby the two men would share the Doves Press type. T. J. Cobden-Sanderson could retain its exclusive use to continue printing as sole proprietor of Doves Press until his death, whereupon ownership of the type would then pass on to the younger man, Emery Walker. Nonetheless, after the Doves Press was closed in 1917, an epitaph appeared in the press's final publication announcing that Cobden-Sanderson had 'bequeathed' the Doves Press Fount of Type to the bed of the River Thames.

In 2013, Robert Green released a digital facsimile of the lost Doves type. However, following the acquisition of a greater range of archive material in 2014, Green began to update his digital version of the typeface. But in order to create a definitive reproduction, he decided that the original metal type — now lying on the riverbed — would have to be examined. In November 2014, Port of London Authority divers directed by Mr Green recovered 151 metal sorts belonging the lost fount from the River Thames. A portion of the type will now be donated to the Emery Walker Trust, where it will be displayed to the general public.

Index

Alam, Lubna, 26
Alexanders-seed, 36
Alexanders, 44, 36
Almonds, 5
Amino acids, 38
Antibiotics, 18
Apple cider vinegar, 12
Aqua omnium florum, 14
Aqua stercoris vaccini
    stillatitia, 14
Arsenic, 3, 5, 6, 20, 30, 32, 45
Arts Catalyst, 1, 48, 49
Austria, 10
Austrian, 14
Balsamic vinegar, 40
Basildon, 8
Bavins, 34
Benfleet, 14
Benzoic acid, 24
Biocides, 18
Bivalve broth, 3, 26
Blackberries, 7, 32, 33
Bottom feeders, 3, 34
Bovril boats, 6, 9
Brown Shrimps, 8
Brown Sugar, 12
Brine, 24
Butter, 20, 28, 33, 34
Caffeine, 16
Canvey, 8
Canvey wick, 44
Caramel colouring, 16
Carbonate, 16
Cargo, 9, 24, 34
China, 34
Chlorothalonil, 18

Cinnamon Oil, 16
Citric acid, 16
CO_2 catridges, 16
Coal, 32, 34, 35, 36
Coal-burner, 35
Coal cargo, 34
Cocklers, 26
Cockles, 7, 26, 28
Cockle sheds, 26
Cola, 16
Common mallow, 44
Crangon crangon, 24
Critical Art Ensemble, 1, 49
Cube-Cola, 16
DCOIT (4,5-dichloro-2-
    n-octyl-4-isothiazolin-
    3-one, Sea-nine 211Â®), 18
Denmark, 10
Diarrhea, 16
Diuron, 18
DIY method, 16
Ecosystem engineers, 26
Elder-trees, 10
Elderflower, 10, 12, 28, 44
Environmental art, 49
Essex, 1, 6, 7, 8, 9, 10, 30,
    34, 48
Eyestalk abalation, 22
Europe, 6, 22
Fennel, 7, 44
Fillet, 36, 42, 43
Fish, 9, 24, 35, 36, 38, 42
Fishing, 24, 34, 38, 42
Fishmongers, 26
Flatulence, 16
Foraging, 8, 20, 30, 32, 44
Freeman, Andy, 1, 48, 49
Gallardo, Fran, 1, 24, 38,
    45, 48, 49
Garlic powder, 40

Goldsmith University, 4
Gout, 14
Grapefruit oil, 16
Greenwich, 34
Grey Mullet, 1, 3, 38,
    40, 42
Grey Mullet Sashimi, 3,
    38, 40
Ground ginger, 40
Gum arabic, 16
Gutweed, 20, 21
Hadleigh Ray, 22, 24
Hairdressers, 38
Hair Soy Sauce, 1, 38, 40
Herring, 7, 34
Hijiki, 20, 21
Hongeohoe, 34
Hungary, 10
India, 26, 34
Invasive Flood, 3, 18
Irgarol 1051, 18
Isomalt, 16
Japanese, 20, 44
Japanese knotweed, 44
Juniper, 44
Kendall, Mikki, 18
Kent, 6, 10, 34
Kosher, 45
L-cysteine, 40, 38
Laver, 20, 21
Leigh-on-Sea, 1, 7, 26,
    32, 38, 49
Lemon Oil, 16
Lemons, 12
Lime Oil, 16
London, 6, 7, 9, 32, 34,
    38, 48, 49
Malaysia, 26
Marigold, 14
Marjoram, 44

Marmite, 14
Marshes, 6, 8, 14, 30, 33
Marsh samphire, 32
Mitten crabs, 18
Mohammed, Che Abd
	Rahim, 26
Mollusc, 18
Molluscs, 26
Moroccan Dirham
	(MAD), 24
Moroccan factory, 24
Morocco, 22, 24
Mud, 3, 7, 14, 16, 24, 30,
	32, 33, 42, 45, 48
Mud Cola, 14, 16
Mudflats, 30
Mugwort, 44
Mushroom, 10
Mycobacterium vaccae, 14
Native Seaweeds, 21
Net, 24, 34, 38, 42
Netherlands, 10
Neurochemical receptors, 5
New Zealand, 26
Norepinephrine, 14
Oil refinery, 44
Old Leigh, 38
Olives, 21
Onion, 20
Orange Oil, 16
Oranges, 12
Oyster, 7, 49
Peel, 20, 22, 24, 36
Phosphoric Acid, 16
Phytoremediation, 32
Pignut, 44
Pimento Filling, 21
Plankton, 26
Polonium, 26
Potatoes, 20

Prozac, 14
Puff, 44
Ramsons, 44
Rheumatism, 14
Salad, 6, 30
Salicornia, 30, 32
Salt marshes, 8, 33
Samphire, 8, 28, 30, 32,
	33, 45
Sashimi cutting, 43
Scrimshaw, Dr. Mark,
	1, 48
Sea aster, 7, 8, 32, 33,
	36, 44, 45
Sea coal, 3, 34
Sea purslane, 8, 32, 33, 45
Seaweed, 20, 21
Sesame Seeds, 20, 21
Serotonin, 14
Shrimp, 3, 8, 22, 24
Shrimping, 24
Skate, 34, 35, 36
Skinning, 43
Slovenia, 26
Sodium Alginate, 21
Sodium Benzoate, 16
Sodium Citrate, 16
Soda syphon, 16
Sorbic acid, 24
Soup, 18, 20, 21
South-East, 14
Southend, 6, 12, 24, 26,
	32, 48, 49
Souvenir, 38
Sprats, 34
saprophytic, 14
SSSI (Site of Specific
	Scientific Interest),
	30, 45
Sting rays, 34

Suffolk, 6, 34
Sugar, 12, 16
Syphilis, 32
Tanger, 24
Tétouan, 24
TCMS pyridine
	(2,3,3,6-tetra-
	chloro-4-methylsulfo-
	nyl pyridine), 18
Thailand, 22
Thames Estuary, 1, 5, 6,
	9, 30, 32, 34, 40, 44, 49
Tongue, 1, 5, 8, 9, 22, 48, 49
Tributyltin (TBT), 18
Tsing, A. C., 10
Tuberculosis, 14
Two Tree Island, 1, 7, 8,
	9, 16, 30, 33, 42, 45
Umami flavour, 38
Unnatural, 1
Vape, 3, 45, 44
Vegetable glycerin, 52
Vertical Commons, 6,30
Vegetable stock, 20
Vinegar, 3, 6, 12, 28, 30,
	33, 40
Wakame, 18, 20, 21
Wales, 26
Weeds, 30, 44
Welsh coast, 21
White pepper, 40
Whiting, 34
Winter of Discontent, 7
Wild meadow flowers, 14
Wild rose, 44
The Women's Institution
	(WI), 12
Yolke, 26
Zinc pyrithione, 18
Zineb, 18